The Osbournes

DAVID KATZ AND MICHAEL ROBIN

A ROUNDTABLE PRESS BOOK

**Andrews McMeel
Publishing**

Kansas City

ISBN: 0-7407-3165-3

Library of Congress Control Number: 2002106059

FOR ROUNDTABLE PRESS, INC.
Directors: Julie Merberg and Marsha Melnick
Executive Editor: Patty Brown
Editor: Sara Newberry
Assistant Editor: Alison Volk

Design by Charles Kreloff

02 03 04 05 06 RR2 10 9 8 7 6 5 4 3 2 1

ATTENTION: SCHOOLS AND BUSINESSES
Andrews McMeel books are available at quantity discounts with bulk purchase for educational, business, or sales promotional use. For information, please write to: Special Sales Department, Andrews McMeel Publishing, 4520 Main Street, Kansas City, Missouri 64111.

PHOTO CREDITS: page 1, Kate Lilienthal/Splashnews.com; page 2, Mark Seliger/Corbis Outline; page 5, Tony Mott/S.I.N./Corbis; page 7 left, Ron Sachs/Corbis Sygma; page 7 right, Ron Sachs/Corbis Sygma; page 9, WireImage; page 11, WireImage; page 12, Neal Preston/Corbis; page 15, Ross Marino/Corbis Sygma; page 17, Photofest; page 18, WireImage; page 21, Globe Photos; page 22, WireImage; page 25, GEMS/Redferns/Retna; page 27, WireImage; page 29, WireImage; page 31, Mark Seliger/Corbis Outline; page 32, Photofest; page 33, Ross Marino/Corbis Sygma; page 35, Lynn Goldsmith/Corbis; page 37, Neal Preston/Corbis; page 39, Neal Preston/Corbis; page 40, Neal Preston/Corbis; page 41, Neal Preston/Corbis; page 43, Neal Preston/Corbis; page 45, George Bodnar/Retna; page 46, Jeff Spicer/Globe Photos; page 47, WireImage; page 48, WireImage; page 51, Tom Wagner/Corbis SABA; page 53, Steve Granitz/Retna; page 54, Tom Vickers/Splashnews.com; page 55, Peter Mazel/Sunshine/Retna; page 57, WireImage; page 59, WireImage; page 60, WireImage; page 61, WireImage; page 63, Mark Mainz/Getty Images; page 64, Hank Parker/Corbis Sygma; page 65, Milan Ryba/Globe Photos; page 66, Gregory Pace/Corbis Sygma; page 67, WireImage; page 69, WireImage; page 71, John Barrett/Globe Photos; page 73 top left, Fin Costello/Redferns/Retna; page 73 top right, Globe Photos; page 73 bottom left, Ross Marino/Retna; page 73 bottom right, Mick Hutson/Redferns/Retna; page 74, WireImage; page 77, Lynn Goldsmith/Corbis; page 78, Mark Seliger/Corbis Outline; page 81, Rick Mackler/Globe Photos; page 82, Jeff Minton/Corbis Outline; page 85, Doug S. Ordway/Corbis Outline; page 86, Neal Preston/Corbis; page 87, Mick Hutson/Redferns/Retna; page 89, Jeff Minton/Corbis Outline; page 91, Rufus F. Folkks/Corbis; page 92, WireImage; page 95, Reuters NewMedia Inc./Corbis; page 96, WireImage

"Of all the things I've lost,
I miss my mind the most."

MAY 4, 2002

Scene: the eighty-eighth annual White House Correspondents' Dinner, an event attended by the biggest names in politics, news, and entertainment. Superstars as diverse as Harrison Ford and Colin Powell were practically trampled as guests strained for a look at the improbable figure at table 168.

Who was it that eclipsed the brightest lights of politics and culture? It doddered unsteadily, but it wasn't Strom Thurmond. It wore the ghoulish cast of a creature from beyond the grave, but it wasn't Strom Thurmond. It publicly pawed the breasts of its female companion, but, no, it wasn't Strom Thurmond. America's first family was being upstaged on its home turf by the head of television's first family—Ozzy Osbourne.

Host Drew Carey couldn't resist commenting, "You know, Ozzy and the president actually have a lot in common. They both love their families, both partied a little too hard when they were younger, half the time you can't understand a word either one of them is saying, and neither one of them can make a move without their wife's approval."

As flashbulbs popped, Sharon Osbourne leaned over to her husband. "Open your mouth wide," she ordered. He immediately complied.

President Bush presented a slide show that included a photo that seemed to show Vice President Dick Cheney urinating on the Oval Office door. The joke was partially intended for Ozzy, who was once interviewed by the FBI for allegedly threatening to do that very thing! The crowd at the Correspondents' Dinner went crazy (by D.C. standards) when Osbourne stood up on his chair and waved. President Bush conceded, "Okay, Ozzy . . . might have been a mistake."

Ozzy and the president even found time for a private chat. "You should wear your hair like mine," suggested Ozzy, indicating his long magenta-highlighted mane. President Bush laughed and replied, "Second term, Ozzy!"

The leader of the free world and the prince of bleeping darkness sharing grooming tips? How did it ever come to this?

SHARON AND OZZY AT THE 88TH ANNUAL
WHITE HOUSE CORRESPONDENTS' DINNER

Sharon doesn't need plastic surgery to lift her breasts– Ozzy'll do it!

IN ✝HE BEGINNING

John Michael "Ozzy" Osbourne came into this world on December 3, 1948, already an unholy howling terror. The unsuspecting midwife would have the privilege of being the first to see the "godfather of heavy metal" in the pose that would make him famous: fingers clawed, mouth wide open, letting out an earsplitting wail. One imagines Ozzy's mother, Lillian, smiling like Mia Farrow in *Rosemary's Baby*, unaware of what she's just unleashed upon the world.

How best to characterize the early years of young John Michael Osbourne? Put it this way: Ever seen *The Omen*? In Ozzy's own words: "I was the worst kid on the face of the earth." True? You decide.

Growing up in the Aston section of Birmingham, England, Ozzy enjoyed a boy's usual interests: *Lassie, I Love Lucy,* the occasional barn burning. With six children crammed into a single bedroom, there was bound to be friction. And as anyone who's rubbed two sticks together knows, friction produces sparks: Ozzy once tried to set his sister on fire! He has also credited himself with other solutions to the overcrowding problem: trying to strangle his brother, murder his mother, and hang himself. Ozzy's boyish high jinks usually earned him a sound beating from his father, Jack. However, Jack could be unpredictable: Once Ozzy

OZZY CIRCA 1970S

confessed to blackening his sister's eyes and Jack unexpectedly retorted, "Good. About time you bleeping whacked her." No wonder the modern-day Ozzy keeps an even temper at home—compared with his own antics, Kelly's and Jack's are no big deal!

Sadly, photographs of Ozzy's childhood are scarce. He claims his sister once took a scissors and cut the heads off everyone in the family album. Apparently you don't need a photo to see the resemblance. Ozzy readily admits, "My whole family's bleeping nuts."

Still, Ozzy credits his parents for shaping his future interests: "My mother was an amateur singer; my father was an amateur drunk." He'd eventually surpass each in their respective fields.

Ozzy's father worked nights in a steel plant, and his mother worked days in an auto assembly plant. While the children never lacked food, they had to go without almost everything else. "We lived on nothing" is how Ozzy describes it. He used a bucket for a toilet and an overcoat for bedclothes. Although these days his daughter complains that he runs around the house in his underwear, she shouldn't blame him for wanting to show it off; in childhood, he couldn't afford any underwear at all.

Ozzy remembers listening to his parents fight about money. "I used to sit on the front steps all the time and think, 'One of these days I'm going to buy a Rolls-Royce and drive them out of this shithole.'"

Educating Ozzy

But the road out of Aston remained unclear. Ozzy and school were never a good match. "I couldn't understand what the bleep the teacher was writing," he says. His dyslexia and attention deficit disorder wouldn't be diagnosed until adulthood. Classmates called him "Ozzy" because of his last name. The nickname stuck. These days, he reportedly doesn't even react when somebody calls him "John." Of course, some days he doesn't even react when somebody calls him "Ozzy," but that's another story.

Among Ozzy's tormentors was his future Black Sabbath band mate Tony Iommi. The chemistry between them was obvious from the start. "I couldn't stand him," recalls Tony. "He was a little punk." Tony and his friends would mock Ozzy's voice, saying it sounded like a girl's. Little did Tony know that that voice would one day help make them both famous.

Ozzy and his two sisters, Hollywood, California, April 2002

OZZY, LONG BEACH, CALIFORNIA, SEPTEMBER 1975

Ozzy the Plumber?

Thrown out of school at fifteen, Ozzy tried to earn an honest living. Jobs as a plumber's assistant and a toolmaker's apprentice went nowhere. He spent two years in a slaughterhouse; perhaps some dark corner of his mind surveyed the gore and thought, *Stage props!*

A lot about Ozzy's taste in music can be traced to his job tuning horns in a car factory. He'd stand in a soundproof booth, blowing and adjusting horns as they arrived on a conveyor belt. One day Ozzy asked a colleague how long he'd worked there. When told thirty-five years, Ozzy flung down his tools. "If I want a bleeping gold watch," he announced, "I'll go and break [into] a jewelry shop." It's a good thing Ozzy succeeded as a rock star—he was a terrible criminal! He once tried to sneak off with a television set and wound up dropping it on himself. He was clever enough to wear gloves while breaking and entering, but not clever enough to make sure the gloves had fingers. Next stop: Winson Green Prison.

While Ozzy often recalls his father's rage over Ozzy's first tattoo, he neglects to mention that Jack may have had other reasons to be irritated: Ozzy acquired his first tattoo behind bars. He did the artwork himself, tattooing smiley faces onto both knees and the now-famous "OZZY" onto the knuckles of his left hand, with a sewing needle and a piece of graphite.

Ozzy, the Fifth Beatle?

Ozzy's life changed when he heard the Beatles for the first time. The lad who'd dreamed of being a plumber now set his sights elsewhere. "That's my way out," he thought. "My music."

Ozzy remains a Beatles fanatic to this day, naming *Rubber Soul, Revolver, Sgt. Pepper's Lonely Hearts Club Band*, and *The White Album* among his favorites. Surprisingly, the godfather of heavy metal even likes Paul McCartney's solo material, despite its saccharine reputation. Ozzy was thrilled to finally meet Paul this year. Ozzy's even expressed admiration for Phil Collins and Culture Club. His affinity for Pat Boone begins to seem less and less peculiar.

Ozzy admits that he doesn't listen to as much contemporary music as he should. He thinks most of today's music lacks melody. A notable exception is the band Creed, which he praises, though his consistent "classic" standbys remain the Beatles, along with Led Zeppelin and David Bowie's *Ziggy Stardust*.

At the time he embarked upon a career in music, Ozzy's biggest gig was a school production of *The Pirates of Penzance*. History fails to record whether or not he threw cow parts during that one. But Ozzy's dad supported his son's dream by buying him a microphone and a small amplifier. The world would never be the same.

Ozzy pinned an ad to a music shop wall that read OZZY ZIG REQUIRES GIG. Why he invented the soon-to-be-discarded last name *Zig* is unclear—the smart money says Ozzy needed something to rhyme with *gig*. One of the musicians who responded was neighborhood social outcast Terence "Geezer" Butler. When you're in a band with Ozzy and *you're* the social outcast, you know you're in trouble. Ozzy teamed up with Geezer either because he sensed promising musical synergy or because he sensed that there's a lot of fun to be had with a guy named Geezer. Whatever the reason, Ozzy's instinct paid off.

Two other musicians who answered Ozzy's ad were drummer Bill Ward and Ozzy's old schoolyard nemesis, guitarist Tony Iommi. Ozzy eventually agreed to join up with Bill and Tony, on the condition that there be no noogies during rehearsal.

Naming the Band

Ozzy, Tony, Geezer, and Bill started rehearsing other bands' songs and named themselves Polka Tulk. Eventually someone noticed that Polka Tulk sounds like a dance the Poles taught the Native Americans, so they changed the name to something less obscure: Earth. In a way it's a shame; MTV could have gotten an entire season out of Ozzy trying to pronounce Polka Tulk.

Unfortunately for Ozzy and friends, there was already a band named Earth—one with an upscale following and a very different sound. Their first clue that something was amiss came when they were asked to perform in tuxedos. It would have been worth the price of admission just to watch Ozzy try to put on a bow tie. Their next clue was the sea of aghast faces that constituted their audience. Spend enough time staring into the angry faces of another band's fans and even a guy named Geezer understands there's a problem. Back to the old drawing board.

Some time earlier, the band had written their first original song and named it after a Boris Karloff movie. After the Earth debacle, the name of the song became the name of the band: Black Sabbath.

The Thinking Man's Guide to Ozzy's Tattoos

Right arm:

Rose with Sharon's name beneath it on the shoulder

Snarling helmeted demon atop an arm-length "sleeve" of symbols and flames

"Mom" and "Pop"

The number 3—or is it the letter *m*?

The word "THANKS" on the right palm—an ever-ready acceptance speech?

Chest:

Flaming blue dragon on the right side

Red-hooded fanged skull on the left side

Left arm:

Bat atop a vampiric woman's head on the shoulder

Dagger through Ozzy banner on inner arm

Skull with a knife through it on inner arm

Stick man on left wrist just below the thumb

"OZZY" on left-hand knuckles

Below the belt:

Sword through a heart on the right thigh

Smiley faces on both knees

BLACK SABBA✝H

Black Sabbath's MVP in those days? No contest: Tony's mom. Mrs. Iommi gave the boys a van, chocolate, and cigarettes—all the rock 'n' roll food groups. The band tore from club to club, hoping an act wouldn't show up so they could go on. It was a time of enormous struggle and creativity. Ozzy once poured purple paint over himself during a show to grab the audience's attention. It didn't work. Maybe that's when he first considered upgrading to blood. If all else failed, the band turned up the volume until they'd drowned out every conversation in the room.

In a happy accident, Tony Iommi cut off his fingertips at his factory job. Undeterred, he capped the stubs with thimbles and loosened his guitar strings so they'd be easier to play. The resulting low, sludgy rumble was a perfect match for Ozzy's wail and Geezer's dark poetry. Slowly but surely, the boys from Birmingham were redefining rock and roll.

"We were completely surrounded by violence and pollution," says Tony, explaining Sabbath's sound. "We were living our music."

For a guy with a devil head on his door, Ozzy has spent a lot of time denying a connection to Satanism. Back in the Black Sabbath days, those misled included actual Satanists. The band once refused an invitation to play a Satanists' convention at Stonehenge. Perhaps warming up a crowd for Satan seemed redundant? When the Satanists retaliated with a hex, Ozzy turned to a higher power: his dad.

Jack made the band aluminum crosses and they wore them all day long. Ozzy continues to collect crosses to this day.

Black Sabbath's first album was released in 1970, fittingly enough on Friday the thirteenth. The company that released it insisted on putting an upside-down cross on the cover. The band's evil reputation was assured.

Ozzy raced to his parents' house with his newly released record. He hadn't yet heard the final product himself. One can only imagine the heartwarming scene: The family gathered 'round the phonograph, Ozzy caterwauling about evil

TONY "STUBBY" IOMMI

and death. When Ozzy's dad finally spoke, it wasn't the response Ozzy was looking for. "Are you sure you were only drinking alcohol?" he asked. "This isn't music. . . . This is weird!"

Nevertheless, when Ozzy received his first royalty check, he bought himself only shoes and cologne, then gave the rest to his mother. Maybe if Dad's review had been kinder, he, too, would have gotten a cut.

Parents everywhere agreed with Jack's verdict. It didn't matter. Although recorded in just eight hours and rejected by over a dozen labels, Black Sabbath's first album reached number eight in the United Kingdom. Like some terrifying beast rising from the muck and taking its first thunderous steps on land, Black Sabbath was beginning to hit its stride.

With the album came the band's first tour. An ocean away, people began battening down the hatches. The beast was coming to America.

The Beast Arrives

Black Sabbath was onstage at New York's Fillmore East, and Ozzy was getting frustrated. What was wrong with these Yanks? Sabbath was blowing the roof off, but the audience just sat there. Ozzy shouted at them to go crazy, but they turned a deaf ear. Given the band's volume, this was perhaps literally true. Finally, a frustrated Bill Ward threw his drum kit into the crowd. The fans went wild and demanded seven encores. Ozzy's conclusion? "I think America likes aggression." Sabbath's foothold in the United States was assured.

Ozzy developed a reputation for urging audiences into frenzies. If an audience dissatisfied him, he'd unleash a stream of abuse. Ozzy has unleashed worse streams upon fans—reportedly once urinating upon their unsuspecting heads—so the recipients of verbal abuse got off easy.

At times, audiences abused Sabbath right back. When the "Paranoid" single climbed the charts in 1970, wildly excited fans were known to storm the stage. On at least one occasion they rampaged and trashed the band's equipment. Worse, the band was once attacked and beaten by a gang of skinheads. Sabbath later mocked their assailants with the song "Fairies Wear Boots."

Late 1970 saw the release of *Paranoid*, an album that showcases Black Sabbath at the height of their powers. Classics abound: "War Pigs," "Iron Man," "Paranoid." Ozzy still names these among the songs of which he's proudest.

Ozzy was living his dream, a dream that included enormous helpings of sex, drugs, and booze. "I can do nothing in moderation," Ozzy admits. "If it's booze, I drink the place dry. If it's drugs, I take everything and then scrape the carpet for little crumbs." He and his band mates relished their reputations as world-class car wreckers and hotel room trashers.

Osbournes fans know that Ozzy had a urinal installed in his Beverly Hills bathroom because of his bad aim. Must be the shaky hands. But Tony Iommi recalls a time when Ozzy decided to move his bowels in the elevator of a swanky hotel. The doors opened in the lobby and the well-heeled guests beheld the godfather of heavy metal with his pants around his knees. Now that, folks, is bad aim.

Ozzy took a good look at himself and decided there was only one thing to do: get married.

The Not-Ready-for-Primetime Marriage

Yes, there was an Osbourne family that never made it to television. Picture the expression on five-year-old Elliot Mayfair's face the day his mother, Thelma, brought his new stepfather Ozzy home. Ozzy's first marriage produced two children: Jessica Starshine in 1973 and Louis in 1974. How much time the children spent bouncing on Ozzy's smiley-faced knees is unclear; between the demands of superstardom and addiction, he wasn't around much.

Imagine if the cameras had rolled in the 1970s. Ozzy'd still be chasing cats around the yard, only he'd have a shotgun in one hand and a butcher knife in the other. That's what he was holding the day Thelma came home and found him passed out beneath the piano, having slaughtered the family's seventeen cats. Clearly Ozzy is more of a dog person.

An episode from 1976: Thelma tells Ozzy it's his turn to feed the chickens. Ozzy ignores her. Thelma keeps bugging him. Aw, they're just like any normal family. Ozzy grabs his shotgun and stomps off to the coop. Looks like leftovers for a month.

The series finale: Ozzy comes home and finds his belongings in the yard. Thelma threatens to have him jailed if he ever enters their house again. It's 1981; the marriage is over. Roll credits.

Fans of *The Osbournes* know that Louis somehow ducked the buckshot and

BLACK SABBATH SOMEWHERE IN THE SEVENTIES

survived to be a frequent guest at his father's Beverly Hills mansion. Louis's debut in the music world came when he appeared on the cover of Ozzy's second solo album, *Diary of a Madman*. Today, he's a techno DJ who has played all over the world and remains based in Ozzy's hometown of Birmingham, England.

Throughout the '70s, Ozzy's professional life remained as turbulent as his personal life. Black Sabbath's Master of Reality tour was dogged by charges of blasphemy, death threats, and the occasional knife-wielding Satanist. Cocaine earned a special thanks credit on the album's sleeve. At the height of his debauchery, Ozzy was rumored to be receiving the drug in laundry detergent boxes. Colors were never brighter.

In 1974, Ozzy fronted Sabbath before a crowd of nearly half a million at the Cal Jam concert in Ontario, California. Not bad for a kid whose first public performance (at the Birmingham firehouse) drew exactly three people. Sabbath's take from the concert may have been as much as $250,000, but band members claimed their managers gave them only $1,000 each. Even though the band ran out of fingers, especially Tony, they were able to do the math. It was time for new management.

Black Sabbath signed with Don Arden, a tough, bare-knuckled manager best known for his work with Electric Light Orchestra. You don't often see the words *tough* and *bare-knuckled* in the same sentence as *Electric Light Orchestra*, but there you have it. It was at Arden's office that Ozzy met the woman who would change his life: Arden's daughter Sharon.

It would be nice to report that Sharon breezed into the room to the strains of Electric Light Orchestra's "Evil Woman" and Ozzy's eyes lit up. However, it was hardly love at first sight. Ozzy came into Don Arden's office wearing a faucet on a chain around his neck and took a seat on the floor. Sharon was so unnerved by

"If I had to start it all over again, the only thing I would change is I'd learn to read a contract better."

her future husband that she almost refused to bring him a cup of tea. Perhaps Ozzy would have noticed her if she'd instead brought him a bucket of blow. But romance remained in the future for the moment.

A reinvigorated Black Sabbath released *Sabbath Bloody Sabbath* in 1974. It was another musical high point—their last. Things were going downhill.

Sabotage, the group's 1975 release, was remarkable only for the ridiculousness of the costumes the band wore on the cover. Guys, we know it was the '70s, but come on. All the controlled substances on the planet can't explain the tights.

Ozzy was devastated by his father's death from cancer in 1977. The song "Junior's Eyes," from *Never Say Die*, which describes a child looking heavenward for answers to his father's death, is Ozzy's moving tribute to the man who gave him his start in life and music.

OZZY'S BLACK SABBATH DISCOGRAPHY

Black Sabbath (1970)

Paranoid (1970)

Master of Reality (1971)

Vol. 4 (1972)

Sabbath Bloody Sabbath (1974)

Sabotage (1975)

We Sold Our Soul for Rock and Roll (greatest hits/1975)

Technical Ecstasy (1976)

Never Say Die (1978)

Ozzy fell into a self-destructive spiral as Black Sabbath prepared to record their next album, *Heaven and Hell*. Ozzy would later admit that he stayed with the band only because he needed money to finance his substance abuse. He'd fail to show up for rehearsals, sometimes vanishing for weeks at a time. He and his band mates were at each other's throats. Something had to give.

In early 1979, it finally did. Ozzy was thrown out of Black Sabbath. He'd later claim he was glad to go, but history suggests otherwise. Ozzy retreated into a motel room and licked his wounds. He probably also licked a lot of mirrors. Drugs and food were delivered. He didn't stir for months. It seemed his career, maybe even his life, was over. He might've died there if it weren't for intervention from an unexpected source.

BLACK SABBATH, 1974

THE BLIZZARD OF OZZ

Sharon Arden had followed her father, Don, into the music business, starting out in her early teens as his receptionist and rising through the ranks. Don was a notorious bully feared throughout the music industry for reportedly using strong-arm tactics like hanging those who displeased him out of windows by their ankles. He was acquitted of charges of false imprisonment and blackmail in 1987. Sharon's brother, David, went to prison for the same charges.

Sharon's business conduct suggests that the acorn didn't drop very far from the tree. The loving mom seen cooing to her pampered puppies on television evidently has a tough-as-nails side rarely seen onscreen. Sharon reportedly once sent Ozzy's old Black Sabbath nemesis, Tony Iommi, a gift-wrapped box of her own feces. A deranged act of vengeance or the perfect gift for the rock star who has everything?

THE BLIZZARD OF OZZ, 1983

27

"If I wasn't doing this, I'd end up either in prison or at the end of a rope."

She once went to the office of a rival company selling unlicensed merchandise and single-handedly trashed their computers. Ironically, Sharon and Ozzy were themselves sued in May 2002 for trademark infringement by a company that claimed the Osbournes stole the idea for a T-shirt that reads !@#$ MY FAMILY, I'M MOVING IN WITH THE OSBOURNES!

Sharon has been known to damage more than property. In early 2002, she was accused of kicking former Ozzy bassist Phil Souzzan in the knee—at a mutual friend's funeral, no less—over a legal dispute. Souzzan got off easy; a promoter who failed to deliver a promised check received Sharon's knee in an even more sensitive portion of his anatomy. Sharon knows that everything in this book is written in a spirit of deep respect and admiration. We pray.

Sharon attributes the mutterings about her character's dark side to rampant music industry sexism. Obviously, no one would think twice if a *man* sent someone his gift-wrapped feces.

When Sharon arrived at Ozzy's motel room in 1979 to collect an old debt, Ozzy was a mess. His life in shambles, his career in ruins, the Oz-man must have been about ready to give up. Sharon wouldn't let him. Instead of hanging Ozzy out the window by his ankles, she convinced him to try a solo career. She persuaded her father, Don, to drop Black Sabbath and stick with Ozzy. Though he couldn't know it at the time, Ozzy had incurred a new debt: He owed Sharon everything.

Sharon would eventually wrest control of Ozzy's management away from her father. The battle created a rift between the hot-tempered Ardens that has never healed. According to the *Guardian*, Don once set his dogs on Sharon during a meeting at his house. Pregnant at the time, she lost the baby. Don has never met Aimee, Kelly, or Jack, and Sharon has vowed that he never will.

Ozzy and Randy in all their glory!

Riding the Crazy Train

Ozzy assembled a new band called Blizzard of Ozz. One of the musicians Sharon lined up to audition was guitarist Randy Rhoads, formerly of Quiet Riot (the band that would later achieve fame with "Cum On Feel the Noize"). The audition lasted just minutes—the man Ozzy would later call "the greatest pure guitarist I ever heard" had the job.

Ozzy had found more than just a guitar player: The two proved to be potent songwriting collaborators. During the Black Sabbath days, Tony and Geezer dominated the songwriting; now Ozzy could finally express himself freely. One of the songs that exploded out of Ozzy and Randy during those heady early days was the classic rock staple "Crazy Train," a lounge version of which opens each episode of *The Osbournes*. Even Kelly names it her favorite of her father's songs.

Contrary to rumor, it is not former Ozzy neighbor Pat Boone's version of "Crazy Train" that plays under the credits. Pat sings his version of the Ozzy classic on *The Osbourne Family Album*. Judging from their divergent musical styles, one would assume that if Ozzy and Pat ever touched they would be mutually annihilated. However, there is nothing but mutual respect between the two men. Pat even has said that he would have done the theme song to *The Osbournes* "for free," but no one ever asked him. An MTV executive has said that he would have loved to have Pat perform the song, but they thought they would never be able to get him.

As the Blizzard of Ozz roared into the '80s, Ozzy would exceed the triumphs of the Black Sabbath era, both in terms of popularity and excess. Sharon, too, became a rising star, admired for her ferocity as a negotiator and her resourcefulness as a promoter.

One of Sharon's best-known promotion efforts is the one that went most drastically awry. Sharon wanted Ozzy to make a memorable entrance at their introductory meeting with CBS Records executives. Ozzy was given live doves and instructed to release them as he entered the conference room. But Ozzy showed up drunk and instead decided to bite a dove's head off. The executives sat

OZZY AND PAT BOONE—PERFECT NEIGHBORS

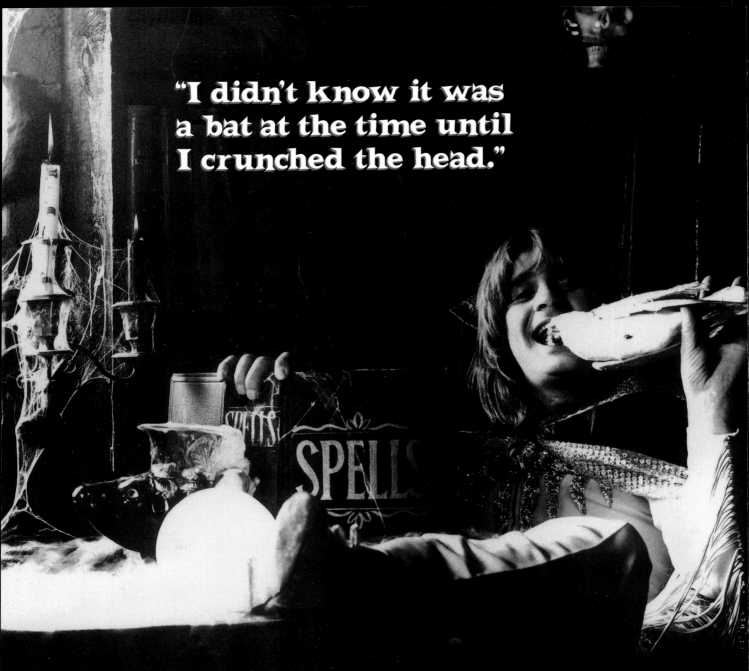

thunderstruck as their new act smiled and spit out feathers. Sharon laughed so hard that she peed in her pants. "It wasn't just a little bit," she recalls. "It was a puddle!" Just to show that it wasn't an accident, Ozzy snacked on a second dove on his way out and threw the carcass at a receptionist. To this day, the fate of a rumored third dove remains a mystery.

Ozzy's '80s concerts were the heavy metal equivalent of Sherman's March. Cities trembled at Ozzy's approach; devastation followed in his wake. Audiences screamed their appreciation.

Sharon has described her husband, like their daughter Kelly, as "accident prone." In the early '80s, *entire tours* were accident-prone. The 1981–82 Diary of a Madman tour was nicknamed the "Night of the Living Dead" tour because of an endless parade of misfortunes. Prop trucks crashed and a falling crane squashed thousands of dollars' worth of equipment.

Ozzy strode across a set that looked like a fog-shrouded castle, attended by a dwarf named John Allen. Although persons of less-than-generous stature have remained an Ozzy concert staple—witness Santa's helpers on the Merry Mayhem tour depicted on *The Osbournes*—none got a worse deal than John Allen, who was flogged with pig intestines and hung from a fake noose. It's a living.

Sharon's negotiations for the Diary of a Madman tour must have been interesting. Ozzy's contract reputedly called for twenty-five pounds of raw meat to be hurled into the audience at every show. The lad who had once handled cow guts in a slaughterhouse was now pitching them into the faces of grateful fans. A young boy's dream of being just like Paul McCartney had finally come true! Delighted young people would return home spattered with blood. Their parents presumably did not become Ozzy fans.

Audiences caught on and began to throw meat back at Ozzy. Fans even smuggled dead animals into the arenas to throw onstage. Security guards once turned away a man attempting to bring in an entire ox head. It's said that a fan once tossed a doll at Ozzy and he panicked, thinking it was a real baby.

At a January 20, 1982, concert in Des Moines, Iowa, a fan threw a live bat onto the stage and Ozzy snatched it up. He would later claim that he thought it was a rubber toy. Most of us would make certain that the object in our hands isn't a live bat before putting it in our mouths, but not our hero. He went ahead and bit the head off. Now that's entertainment.

Sharon had Ozzy rushed to the hospital. He'd earned himself an agonizing series of rabies shots and the enmity of the ASPCA and bats everywhere. Stagehands later looked for the bat but it was nowhere to be found. Somewhere a custodian is smacking his forehead. Imagine what that thing would be worth on

"You see far more violence in a Tom and Jerry cartoon than you see at an Ozzy Osbourne concert."

eBay. Presumably no one volunteered to search Ozzy's stool. Maybe it wound up with Tony Iommi.

Later that year, Ozzy would try to mend fences with a large donation to the ASPCA. It didn't take. Animal rights activists would picket his performances for years to come.

Remember the Alamo

It's long been the perfect Ozzy anecdote: Ozzy went to Texas and peed on the Alamo. The Diary of a Madman tour was in San Antonio. It had been a month since Ozzy had done anything legendarily idiotic, so he was due. In an effort to keep Ozzy out of trouble, Sharon locked away his clothes. Undaunted, Ozzy squeezed into one of Sharon's evening dresses and went out for a bottle of booze. When nature called, he lifted his skirts and marked his territory . . . right on the Alamo's walls. When it comes to Bowies, Ozzy evidently respects David more than Jim. At some point, perhaps during the writing of the second z, the cops were called and Ozzy got his first taste of Lone Star justice: He was arrested and banned from San Antonio! Eventually Ozzy set things right with a donation to the Alamo's caretakers and, after a decade in exile, he was welcomed back.

This era's darkest episode took place outside Leesburg, Florida, during the early morning hours of March 19, 1982. While Ozzy and Sharon slept in their idling tour bus, driver Andrew Aycock commandeered a single-engine airplane and took Ozzy's guitarist and songwriting collaborator, Randy Rhoads, and another crew member for a joyride. Aycock, his pilot's license invalid and cocaine in his system, buzzed the tour bus three times, then dove straight at it. Some have speculated that Aycock's target was his ex-wife, Wanda, who was traveling with the band. The plane sliced through the bus, narrowly missing Ozzy and Sharon, then plowed into a garage and exploded. Ozzy and Sharon felt the impact and rushed out to find the garage and adjacent house in flames. Everyone aboard the plane was dead.

Some have credited Ozzy with racing into the burning house and rescuing a deaf man who didn't know anything had happened. Why, in a burning house that has just been hit by a plane, one would need the sense of hearing in order to detect something amiss is a question for wiser heads.

Ozzy has been steadfast in his efforts to help keep Randy Rhoads's memory alive. He's built Randy a tomb and sends flowers to it every year. In 1987, on the anniversary of the plane crash that took Randy's life, Ozzy released the Randy Rhoads *Tribute* album. But perhaps the legacy that would please Randy most is the music itself. Their collaborations have proven immortal. At this very moment, "Crazy Train" is blasting out of speakers all over the world.

RANDY RHOADS, 1981

⊕ZZY AND SHAR⊕N

The year 1982 was not defined only by tragedy and mishap. On July 4, Ozzy Osbourne and Sharon Arden were married in Maui. Why July 4? Ozzy wanted a date that would be easy to remember. What a romantic!

Ozzy told *Osbournes* audiences that the thing that first attracted him to Sharon was her laugh. Her tendency to laugh when he does things that send everyone else fleeing in horror was undoubtedly a bonus. For her part, Sharon asserts that Ozzy's lack of pretension set him apart from the artists by whom she'd been surrounded since childhood. Besides, she adds, "He was gorgeous."

Sharon recalls how no one expected her and Ozzy to last. "They expected him to have a big-titted blonde trophy wife and he'd got me, a short, fat, hairy half-Jew." Maybe Sharon's brilliance at promotion is limited to rock bands.

On September 2, 1983, Ozzy and Sharon's first daughter, Aimee Rachel, was born. She was followed on October 27, 1984, by sister Kelly Lee. Jack made his debut November 8, 1985. The children's births were bright spots in an increasingly chaotic decade.

During the early '80s, Sharon's excesses rivaled Ozzy's. She has confessed to a

weakness in those days for Quaaludes and alcohol. If you think two combustible personalities and loads of intoxicants sounds like a formula for trouble, you're right; Ozzy and Sharon's fights were the stuff of legend. *Osbournes* fans who chuckled over Sharon's playful poke at Ozzy's eye on the tour bus should know that, given this couple's history, that was a little like the United States playfully lobbing a missile into Moscow.

"We'd beat the shit out of each other" is how Sharon remembers the old days. Ozzy would run offstage during guitar solos to fight with her, then run back to the microphone to finish the song. Their increasingly "Sid and Nancy"–like relationship seemed headed for calamity.

When Sharon woke up one day with no memory of her drunken driving arrest the night before, she finally got the message. Unless something changed, she and Ozzy were headed for the gutter. Although Sharon finally got serious about sobering up, it would be years before Ozzy followed suit. For the sake of the children, she was determined to stick with the marriage.

Although these days Ozzy exclaims over a litter of cigarette butts after Kelly's birthday party, his squeamishness is definitely a recent development. One festive moment during his early '80s tour with Mötley Crüe saw Ozzy down on his knees snorting a line of ants. Now that's a stimulant!

"My kids do not sleep in the attic, hanging upside down on rafters."

Television audiences were shocked when Sharon threatened to urinate in unwanted houseguest Jason Dill's whiskey bottle, but, in the Osbourne household, urine may be considered a potable beverage. In wilder days, Ozzy was said to occasionally drink his own. Considering Ozzy's habits at the time, the stuff was probably eighty proof. But, hey, look on the bright side: Ozzy recycles!

Sharon's resolve to salvage her marriage was dramatically tested on many occasions. One night she flew to Japan to meet Ozzy on tour and waited for him in their hotel room bed. Finally someone crept into the darkened room and joined Sharon beneath the sheets. Only it wasn't Ozzy! It was a Japanese groupie that the drunken Ozzy had brought back for a romp . . . forgetting that Sharon had arrived earlier that day! If some optimistic voice in Ozzy's addled rock-star brain whispered *threesome*, Sharon dispelled the notion by throwing the groupie bodily from the room and then letting her husband have it. If that moment had been filmed for television, the number of bleeps would have set records.

Ozzy and Sharon's lowest point came on September 2, 1989. Ozzy opened a crate of vodka he'd received, ironically enough, at a Moscow peace festival, downed several bottles, and decided to strangle Sharon. He wrapped his fingers around her throat, declaring "We've decided you have to go." Sharon hit a panic button that summoned the police and Ozzy was taken into custody. He woke up the next day with no memory of what he'd done. Sharon didn't press charges, but Ozzy was forced into rehab for three months. The ugliness of this episode made an impression even on the incorrigible Ozzy. Though it would be a continual struggle, he battled and ultimately contained his addictions. These days, he's even off cigarettes.

Sharon has described Ozzy in the '80s as a sort of Jekyll and Hyde: a loving father and husband while sober and an abusive terror during the inevitable benders. As Ozzy gradually freed himself from addiction, the vicious side receded. Sharon's faith was rewarded. Perhaps now, a more accurate horror film metaphor

SHARON, OZZY, KELLY, AND AIMEE, 1984

to describe Ozzy would be a lumbering, dazed Frankenstein monster (Sharon being Dr. Frankenstein, of course). To this day they smooch publicly with the enthusiasm of newlyweds, much to Kelly's and Jack's dismay. That embarrassment pales beside the horror that led Jack to jam his fingers in his ears on an *Osbournes* episode: Ozzy, on *Loveline*, telling a story about waiting for his Viagra to kick in and finding himself stuck "camping with a tentpole" when Sharon dozed off.

Ozzy has mended fences beyond his family. He has reunited with Black Sabbath on several occasions. In an alliance once thought even more unthinkable, Ozzy recently teamed up with animal rights activists to protest the mistreatment of cats and dogs in Korea. (Killing them's fine, but eating them!)

Even religious conservatives are beginning to see the light. Former vice president Dan Quayle, who targeted Candice Bergen's decision to have an illegitimate child on her CBS sitcom *Murphy Brown* as an affront to American family values, is the latest to climb aboard Ozzy's crazy train. According to the Associated Press, Quayle said, "In a weird way, Ozzy is a great antidrug promotion. Look at him and how fried his brains are from taking drugs all those years and everyone will say, 'I don't want to be like that.' . . . I think there are some very good lessons there that are being transmitted."

Sobriety has paid off in other ways. Starting with 1991's *No More Tears*, he abandoned the grisly covers and titles that had characterized his albums for years. His song "I Don't Want to Change the World" earned him a Grammy in 1992.

Ozzy reportedly once declared, "I'd rather die than become a boring old fart." It seems as though now he's somewhere in between. Although these days he showers his audiences with water rather than blood, Ozzy still rocks hard. After attempting to retire from the road after 1992's No More Tours tour, he came roaring back in 1996 with the Retirement Sucks tour. Ozzy has vowed that his next retirement will come only when they put him in the ground.

The year 1996 also saw the debut of Ozzfest, one of Sharon's most lucrative brainstorms. Ozzfest came about when the Lollapalooza Festival rejected Ozzy because he wasn't hip enough. Today, Lollapalooza is long defunct and Ozzfest is bigger than ever. Living well is the best revenge!

AIMEE, JACK, OZZY, AND KELLY, 1991

Osbourne-related enterprises have been so successful that Sharon has cut back on her work with other bands. She's turned down requests for her management services from musical heavyweights such as Guns 'n' Roses and Courtney Love. A collaboration with the Billy Corgan–led Smashing Pumpkins fell apart after only three months. Sharon issued a press release, famously declaring that she was forced to withdraw from the arrangement for medical reasons: "Billy Corgan was making me sick."

With the family fortunes at an all-time high, little did the Osbournes suspect that their profile was about to rise in a way they'd never imagined.

OPPOSITE: THE OSBOURNES IN LONDON, 1997
ABOVE: AT THE 42ND ANNUAL GRAMMY AWARDS, LOS ANGELES, CALIFORNIA, 2000

PROLOGUE TO A HIT

"There are no second acts in American lives."
—F. Scott Fitzgerald

(Keep in mind the Osbournes are British.)

The phenomenon of *The Osbournes* has been compared and contrasted with every family sitcom from *Ozzie and Harriet* and *The Munsters* to *The Cosby Show*. MTV itself bills *The Osbournes* as "the next generation of family-oriented sitcom." But the truth is that the most freakish family-centered show in television history can trace its origins to, of all places, the dry corridors of public television programming. In 1973 PBS aired *An American Family*, a vérité series that allowed viewers to follow the daily lives of the Loud family. For the first time in TV history, the everyday activities of "real people" were taped, edited, and aired for all the world to see.

Six years later, comedian and filmmaker Albert Brooks made the cult classic *Real Life,* starring Charles Grodin, a satire of the acclaimed PBS series. *Real Life,* one of the first films later known as "mockumentaries," was a direct forebear of another classic comedy, Rob Reiner's *This Is Spinal Tap*, which followed the day-to-day ups and downs of a band that was partly based on Black Sabbath. So, unsurprisingly, *Spinal Tap* is frequently mentioned as another direct precursor of *The Osbournes.*

It was MTV, with their series *The Real World*, that took it all to the next level of popularity by showing that real life can be more entertaining than fiction. But where *The Real World* blew up normal people into huge celebrities, with *The Osbournes* the formula has been reversed: Viewers were able to see that huge stars, in their daily lives, are really just like all the rest of us (kind of).

The germ of what was to become *The Osbournes* was born when Ozzy and the family were featured on an episode of the MTV series *Cribs*, a hip version of *Lifestyles of the Rich and Famous*. The immediate response was so positive that a reality show based on the family was immediately put into development. The rest is history.

IN ✝HE BEGINNING . . .

**Though a reality show, "The Osbournes"
contains many of the elements of
a classic television sitcom
(as written by David Lynch).**

"What is a functional family? What guidelines do we all have to go by? The Waltons?"

51

LOVING FATHER AND SON

Ozzy and Jack are the Herman and Eddie Munster of the new millennium. Every classic TV show centered on family life has at its center that most special and intimate of relationships, that between a father and a son. "Jack's a very good boy," Ozzy has said. "Compared to me he's an angel. At Jack's age, I was drinking massive amounts of booze, smoking pot, doing speed . . . and I bit several creatures' heads off." Even for a father and son, Ozzy and Jack have a tremendous amount in common. Sometimes their relationship is symbiotic, at other times it's merely parasitic, but you'd have to go as far back as *The Courtship of Eddie's Father* or *Oedipus* to discover such a complex portrayal of the father-son dynamic. It just shows how good television can be if you just take out the writers.

Doing Things Together

What's more American than Pa Walton teaching one of his young sons to hunt? In one episode we see Ozzy giving a thrilled Jack a bayonet that fits his rifle. Clearly this had been an ongoing quest. We all know how frustrating a loose bayonet can be. It's nice when fathers and sons share an interest.

Ozzy and Jack share other interests. On one occasion Jack was blown away when this band he'd never heard of, King Crimson, opened for his beloved Tool. Ozzy played it cool, telling Jack nonchalantly that he'd heard of them, and suggested that if Jack liked King Crimson, he should probably listen to Yes and another band called Gentle Giant. The next day Jack came back to Ozzy and told him he'd listened to the Gentle Giant album. "It's bleeping great music," he said. "How did you know about them?" Ozzy said, "Oh, I've only been around for bleeping thirty-five years!"

OZZY AND JACK, 1991

Dad Needs Technical Assistance

The cry of "Jaaaaaack!" frequently rings out through the Osbourne household. No, it's not a wild animal being attacked; it's the call of a wild animal in need of technical assistance. This sound is heard on many episodes, including when Ozzy can't get his new television set off of the Weather Channel and when he tries to use the DVD player. It's a sad state of affairs, watching Ozzy impotently paw unresponsive controls as he forlornly waits for something to work. You have to wonder what kind of sadists *The Osbournes'* cameramen and crew were. That house was crawling with technical experts. Would it have been so horrible for one of them to reach in a hand, push play for Ozzy, and put him out of his misery? Clearly MTV gave them some kind of reality TV equivalent of *Star Trek*'s prime directive: Do not interfere with the natural development of the alien species.

"Jaaaaaack, how do I turn off the water?"

LIKE FATHER, LIKE KIDS

Hatred for Hippies

Ozzy reacts with disgust when Sharon tells him that campers were singing around the fire every night at a camp they sent Jack to. (Sure, using a fire to summon Satan is okay, but campfire songs? Beyond the pale.) But Ozzy's boy knew how to handle himself when confronted with such horrors; he threw rocks at tents and the other kids and cursed out the counselors. Perhaps Ozzy sent Jack subliminal messages encouraging this behavior by wearing his anti-hippie shirt around the house. It's ironic that in his early Sabbath days, the long-haired Ozzy could have been mistaken for a hippie himself. We don't think he's ever seen an acoustic guitar.

Incontinence

Jack and Ozzy also share a certain casual attitude toward where or when they relieve themselves. Jack has confessed that he wets his bed. (Did Melinda, the nanny, know this when she was hired?) Well, bed-wetting's a nice start, but he has a long way to go until he touches some of Ozzy's widely heralded accomplishments, like defecating in a woman's handbag and on a car.

Drugs

Who can forget that classic *Waltons* episode when Pa told his kids if you do too much coke or pot, let someone else drive the pickup? In this category Ozzy and Jack are closer to the Keatons from *Family Ties* (Dad was an ex-drug-using hippie). Clearly, no one can compete with Ozzy in the drug consumption category and, like most parents, Ozzy is pretty intent on limiting Jack's exploration in that area. When Ozzy learns that Jack has been smoking dope, he says, "You think I don't know what it means when you order a pizza at bleeping twelve o'clock?" Ozzy phones Jack and tries to straighten him out with an old saying: "It's not all fun and no . . . all games and no fun and . . . all fun . . . " Jack has just received a vivid example of the consequences of too much drug fun.

Pratfalls

One of the many traits that Kelly and Ozzy share (along with red-tinted hair), is clumsiness. Ozzy accidentally falling over backward in his chair has become a classic TV moment, right up there with the shooting of J.R. and the Fonz jumping the shark. A less funny and more painful episode was when we see Kelly fall into a hole and injure her foot. Every person that's ever broken a foot falling into a hole has *wished* that a camera crew was there so they could sue for millions. Figures that the one time it happens, it happens to a person who already has millions.

SIBLING RIVALRY

Brothers and sisters quarreling is a sitcom mainstay, as old as *Father Knows Best*, though becoming an art form on *The Brady Bunch*. Of course, *The Osbournes* version is a little more salty than the standard NO GIRLS ALLOWED sign posted to a bedroom door, but Jack and Kelly are the new Bobby and Cindy: Kelly, clearly annoyed that her brother walks around the house in fatigues carrying his rifle, reminds Jack that he once *shot her*. Jack brushes aside her concern. How can she make such a big deal about being hit by a pellet "half the size of a fingernail?" Kelly responds, "It went through my bleeping leg." A football to the nose suddenly seems quaint.

JACK AND KELLY, APRIL 2002

COMING OF AGE
IN FRONT OF THE
CAMERA

Jack

The awkward "coming-of-age" episode is a staple of television shows featuring teenagers. Usually it takes up one episode. With Jack, we've had a full season. We've watched him transform from a chubby, awkward, four-eyed acne-prone misfit into . . . a slightly older chubby, awkward, four-eyed acne-prone misfit. But who cares? According to his mother, he can get a blow job whenever the hell he wants! (Please juxtapose with Mrs. Brady trying to convince Peter he's cute.)

For all the unexpectedly familiar aspects of the Osbournes' household, the children's lifestyles stand out as decidedly, well, different. The largest single factor that may separate the Osbourne kids from the rest of young America is the ability to drop your dad's name to get into the latest club (unless you're a Bush and it's a country club).

Jack's lifestyle, in particular, appears to present him with both privileges and challenges. What kid Jack's age wouldn't want to stay out until all hours, partying and checking out the latest bands? Although he's decided that he needs more experience before starting his own label, Jack remains a scout for Epic and an influential

BLEEPED WORD COUNT

EPISODE ONE: 56
EPISODE TWO: 70
EPISODE THREE: 37
EPISODE FOUR: 62
EPISODE FIVE: 51
EPISODE SIX: 72
EPISODE SEVEN: 54
EPISODE EIGHT: 62
EPISODE NINE: 78
EPISODE TEN: 57

JACK AND KELLY, AUGUST 2001

voice in the selection of bands for Ozzfest; he's the man in charge of selecting acts for the second stage.

But how many other Epic executives spend their summers throwing rocks and being chased by their nannies? If Jack is unique among his professional peers, the same is true with regard to his social peers. Sharon explained on *The Osbournes* that Jack struggles at school and is considered an "oddball." He doesn't socialize with classmates or go to typical hangouts like movies or malls. Any viewer who saw Jack stab a box with a bayonet knows that he enjoys some pastimes that could make the other kids skittish. But who in their right mind would hang out with the local kids at the mall when you could be partying with Slipknot?

Jack's unconventional lifestyle does catch up to him by way of sleep deprivation. Melinda appears to earn most of her paycheck just trying to get Jack out of bed. (He's lucky that this isn't his father's job—back in his day, Ozzy was fond of shaving off people's eyebrows while they slept.) When Sharon asked Melinda if she thought Jack needed to be on antidepressants, Melinda suggested that all Jack required was a good night's sleep. She estimated that he'd had only one in the past two years.

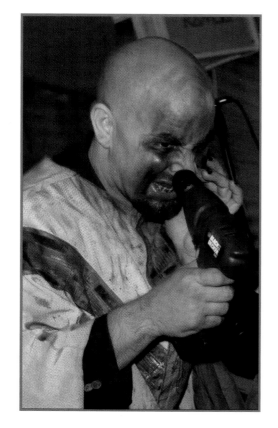

The Osbournes have other reasons for being apprehensive about Jack. Several years ago. while accompanying his father, an *Entertainment Weekly* reporter observed Jack in the catering hall with a performance artist/self-mutilator named Reverend B. Dangerous. Trying to teach Jack some of his tricks, Dangerous was attempting to shove a plastic spoon two inches up Jack's left nostril! He stopped only when Jack

OPPOSITE: JACK, MAY 2002
RIGHT: REVEREND B. DANGEROUS

began to gag. At that time Sharon had already adopted her laid-back parenting technique. She said at the time, "My strategy is not to react, because if I react, he'll only keep doing it."

Jack did succeed in getting a reaction from his mother when a friend gave him a Mohawk before Kelly's birthday party on *The Osbournes*. (Perhaps Sharon worried they'd exposed the 666 behind his ear?) Fans will be interested to know that Jack's interest in hairdo experimentation had already blossomed: Jack once had his head shaved onstage by Methods of Mayhem (featuring Pamela Anderson's infamous ex, Tommy Lee). Sharon was aghast and said her little boy looked like a convict. Considering what a certain video proves Tommy likes to do to shaved objects, Sharon should be happy Jack got off so easy.

Kelly

Ah, the TV parent-daughter relationship. It's usually characterized by tenderness and admiration. But can one picture Bill Cosby and Phylicia Rashad sitting around talking about how they should have named their youngest daughter *Vagina*?

Out of all the Osbournes, it's Kelly who seems most torn between loving the attention that accompanies celebrity status and being uncomfortable with the inconveniences that accompany it (we're not counting Lola, the dog). For instance, at an Ozzy autograph signing at Tower Records, fans awaiting Ozzy's arrival called out to Kelly (maybe they thought she was Belinda Carlisle?) and one fan slipped his arm around Kelly while having a picture taken with her; bodyguards instantly hustled Kelly away. She complains that she "can't stand" being touched by fans. This is an attitude that the normally lenient Sharon will not condone; she does not abide any disrespect for the fans. "I caught the kids giggling once at some Ozzy fans," she said in an interview. "I was so angry. I said to them, 'Don't you ever laugh at those people, because they're the reason we live in the house we do, drive the car we do, and you go to the schools you do. Show some respect.'" You have to admire Sharon's integrity, though Jack and Kelly's position

is understandable; who wouldn't be amused by groupies who are fanatically obsessed and worshipful of a man they see every day walking around in his underwear?

Sharon doesn't defend only Ozzy's fans. Once when she and Ozzy were touring America at the same time as the Spice Girls and staying at the same hotels, they observed the Spice Girls ignoring adoring fans who had been waiting outside. When Sharon saw the heartbroken kids crying, she and Ozzy yelled at the Spice Girls, "You bitches!"

Kelly's desire for attention has also led her into conflict with Jack. At these times they most resemble the kids on *Married with Children*. At one point Kelly whines to her father, "Dad, I hate Jack," and quickly gets into bitching about how she was the one to discover the band Delusion that Jack got a development deal for. She's upset that she never gets any credit. Ozzy suggests that she shouldn't worry about Jack but just do her own thing. Perhaps this advice is what made her decide to focus on her singing career and do a cover of a Madonna hit with the clearly ironic title "Papa Don't

OPPOSITE: KELLY, MAY 2002
RIGHT: OCTOBER 2001

Preach" on *The Osbourne Family Album* CD.

At a news conference Kelly was asked if she had heard from Madonna regarding her rendition of "Papa Don't Preach." Kelly said, "Madonna's been too busy," and then quickly added, "I love her. Who doesn't?" Then Ozzy jumped in. "I don't!" "You just want to bleep her," Sharon suggested. Ozzy demurely responded, "Too old for me." It may have slipped Ozzy's mind that his lovely wife is older than Madonna.

The Normal One

Is there a figure in contemporary pop culture more intriguing than the Osbournes' mysterious eldest daughter, Aimee? The young woman Jay Leno called "the normal girl in the Munster family" moved out of the family home when the cameras moved in (all the way into the guest house). She has continued to protect her privacy even as the show's popularity has exploded. Despite her ambition for a future in music, Aimee even declined

OPPOSITE: KELLY, MARCH 2002
RIGHT: AIMEE, APRIL 2002

"I would hate my children to be the typical rock 'n' roll brats."

an invitation to participate in *The Osbourne Family Album*, suggesting that Kelly sing instead. How did an Osbourne turn out so healthy?

Actually, Aimee's desire to distance herself from the family's media circus predates the MTV show. Years ago, an *Entertainment Weekly* reporter observed the family during a tour and reported that Aimee had been telling bands and crew that she was adopted. At the time an amused Sharon said, "She says her real father is a builder or something. She thinks Ozzy and I are such geeks, she doesn't want to belong to us!"

We know this: Sharon and Kelly are not the only Osbourne females with expensive taste. Four years ago, Aimee paid $16,000 for the privilege of hanging out with the candy-pop band Hanson! The money was in the form of a bid for the City of Hope charity auction in Los Angeles. All that money was just to get Hanson concert tickets, backstage passes, and the opportunity to socialize with the coolest boy group since the Osmonds. According to MTV, Aimee was described as having "a perfect British accent and braces." Sister Kelly is not blameless in this; at the time, Aimee told organizers that she'd be going to the concert with her thirteen-year-old sister.

There are clues to Aimee's nature scattered throughout Season One of *The Osbournes*. Most of these fall into the category of "too much information." For example, it was fine to learn from Kelly that Aimee wears thong underwear every day, but did we really need to know that the Osbourne daughters sometimes share the same pair? Just in case we hadn't connected the dots, Kelly spelled it out: "It's been up my crack, and now it's up her crack, and I'm not down with that." How much would those go for on eBay?

In a similar vein, while it was heartwarming to learn that Aimee looks out for her younger sister, the particulars were not for the faint of heart. When Kelly raged about a call from a woman "telling me how to prepare my vagina," Aimee was to

SHARON AND AIMEE, APRIL 2002

☉ZZY ☉SB☉URNE S☉L☉ DISC☉GRAPHY

Blizzard of Ozz (1981)

Diary of a Madman (1981)

Speak of the Devil (1982)

Live EP (three songs) (1982)

Bark at the Moon (1983)

The Ultimate Sin (1986)

Tribute (1987) (live)

No Rest for the Wicked (1988)

Ten Commandments (1990)
(greatest hits)

Just Say Ozzy (1991) (live)

No More Tears (1991)

Live and Loud (1993) (live)

Ozzmosis (1995)

The Ozzman Cometh (1997)
(greatest hits)

The Ozzfest (1998) (live compilation)

Ozzfest—Second Stage Live (2001)
(live compilation)

Ozzfest—The Second Millenium (2001)
(live compilation)

Down to Earth (2001)

blame. Aimee's efforts to get Kelly a new dentist and a new car along with a new gynecologist are what prompted Kelly to declare, "My teeth, my car, my vagina . . . my business!" She should put that on a mug. It was this involvement in Kelly's affairs that led Ozzy to grow suspicious, wondering why it was that "whenever you mention the vagina doctor you get a smirk on your face." Had Kelly been messing with boys? Or is this just what you get when your daughters share a thong?

We do know that Aimee does show up on video: Look for a glimpse of her face on the left side of the mansion's doorway as Sharon welcomes Ozzy home after his concert injury.

Aimee's absence from the show should in no way be interpreted as estrangement from the family. She is a continual, if rarely photographed, presence at the family's events and her parents and siblings always speak warmly of her (except when she's signing them up for gynecologist appointments). Kelly even predicts she'll join them onscreen in future seasons. It will be that classic television moment: the reunion with the long-lost prodigal child!

LONG-SUFFERING EMPLOYEES

Melinda

Melinda is the Osbournes' Australian nanny. A cross between Alice from *The Brady Bunch* and Daphne from *Frasier*, Melinda was the nanny to the kids when they were younger and Sharon and Ozzy were both busy trying to keep Ozzy's career on track. As time has passed, she has worked more as a personal assistant for the family, but she still oversees the children when Sharon and Ozzy are away. She is also the caretaker of the house and does other odd jobs—none odder than changing Jack's sheets, of course.

The communication between Jack and Melinda is frequently reduced to little more than that versatile Osbourne pleasantry "Bleep you!" Jack won't get out of bed, won't go to school, comes home at all hours, and grouses that having a nanny is childish, and then demonstrates his mastery of adult behavior by spraying Melinda with air freshener.

Michael

No palace is complete without a royal guard. At the Osbourne estate this elite unit was composed of one man: Michael the security guard. He was *The Osbournes'* cross between the mailman on *Mr. Rogers' Neighborhood* and the doorman from *Rhoda*. "Was" is the operative word.

Michael was arrested along with his son for robbing the house behind the Osbournes'.

CRAZY COSTUMES

From *Uncle Miltie* to *The Nanny*, outrageous costume changes have been a staple of TV celebrity. Ozzy's life in rock and roll has uniquely groomed him for this role. During his three-decade career as the king of heavy metal, Ozzy has embraced numerous styles, ranging from British working-class garb to glam rocker getups. *The Osbournes* has given us unprecedented access into the day-to-day events that currently shape Ozzy's "look."

We see what Ozzy does to prepare for a *Tonight Show* appearance: He shows uncharacteristic restraint by turning down lipstick before he performs, then Kelly helps him actually trim some overlong tassles off of his costume.

It becomes clear that, as with every other aspect of Ozzy's life, Sharon has a lot of input when it comes to Ozzy's clothing. At one point, when Sharon is dressing him for an in-store appearance to mark his new album's release, Ozzy frets over the clothes she's picked out: "It's not feminine looking?" a concerned Ozzy asks, eyeing his very feminine looking outfit. Maybe Ozzy should remind her that he was in Black Sabbath, not the Thompson Twins.

On another occasion, a new video shoot directed by Rob Zombie, Ozzy tries on a shirt that has *good* written on one arm and *evil* written down the other, then a wardrobe person holds up a shirt with nifty bat wings. Ozzy, rather disdainful, says he wants to keep it simple. Sharon likes the shirt. Ozzy says he doesn't want to wear it. Sharon asks him to just try it on, assuring him that if he doesn't like it, he can just take it off. Ozzy makes it clear that he's had enough of bats. "It's all my bleeping career is about, is bleeping bats." Geez, and we thought he just ate them. They finally agree to get Ozzy a plain, nonwinged black shirt. Sometimes Ozzy does wear the pants in the family—just never at home.

The fashion accessory that best sums up Ozzy's transformation from heavy metal god to homebody is a birthday present he receives while on tour: a "Prince of Darkness Pooper Scooper" covered with crosses and jewels. No more messy toilet paper for Ozzy.

COMEDIC AFFLICTIONS

Deafness

Often when Ozzy seems distracted or confused, it's not so much due to being "drug addled" as to the fact that he has suffered hearing loss over the years. At one point, after Kelly gets irritated with Ozzy asking her to repeat herself, Ozzy tells her, "You haven't been standing in front of thirty billion decibels for thirty-five years." Proof of Ozzy's exposure to excessive noise levels is even in the law books. Black Sabbath's earsplitting concerts spurred the city of Leeds to enact a ninety-six-decibel law. Any band that played louder would have its amplifiers cut off. Ozzy didn't consider it a good night's work unless Sabbath's amps cut out at least three times.

Learning Disabilities

Ozzy claims to be dyslexic. (Does he think the name of his old band is Htabbas Kcalb?) Ozzy's dyslexia may give him trouble reading books, but not setting them up. In a deal worth over $3 million, the Osbourne family has sold world rights for two books to Simon & Schuster. This book is not one of them. A president there was quoted as saying, "We're bleeping delighted to publish them."

Ozzy has also said, "My concentration span is very short. What do you call that? Whatever." At last he remembers. "Major attention deficit disorder."

THE TONIGHT SHOW WITH JAY LENO, MAY 2002

Substance Abuse

Though Ozzy is currently alcohol- and drug-free (not counting his medication), there have been occasional lapses. At Thanksgiving Ozzy tells the camera that he's on medication (reportedly Vicodin) and should not be drinking, then cheerfully pours himself a glass of wine. If it were a horror movie, that's when the ominous bone-chilling organ chord would play.

Ozzy, the wine having taken effect, stumbles in on the TV-watching Jack and tells him to walk the dog. Jack says that he will, but makes no move, so Ozzy says, "I'll take the dog for the bleeping walk!" Ozzy finally finds a leash and struggles to put it on an apprehensive Lola, who clearly senses danger. Cut to Ozzy staggering down the street, singing, with Lola in tow, the amusing culmination of turkey, red wine, and Vicodin.

Pyromania

In most homes, the father frowns upon starting fires, but when Kelly starts a fire on the stove, Ozzy doesn't get mad; his eyes light up and he congratulates Kelly for starting their new home's first blaze. He may have gone domestic, but he's still the man who used to hold lighters up to hotel fire alarms.

Wacky Neighbors

Another reliable ingredient for the successful sitcom is the wacky neighbor. Well, *The Osbournes* is no exception. Since the next-door neighbors wimped out of tea with Sharon, we'll never know if they enter a room with the élan of, say, *Seinfeld*'s Kramer. However, the cross-fence conversation blew away anything on *Home Improvement*.

When the neighbors blast what Sharon calls "sex-European-dance-bleeping-shit" in the middle of the night, she finally loses control altogether, throws her

legs into the air, and jams Jack's teddy bear into her crotch. "No!" screams Jack. "That's my bear!" Now the teddy bear is *really* something to tease Jack about. Sharon goes to the neighbors' fence and trades insults. They call her the Wicked Witch of the East, and she replies, "Darling, the Wicked Witch has nothing on me." Jack's teddy bear will back her up on that one!

On another occasion, when "The Girl from Ipanema" blares on the other side of the fence, it's Ozzy's turn to snap. How much can a heavy metal god take? "If they want a bleeping war, we'll give them one," he snarls. Jack, excited by all this war talk, enthusiastically agrees. Somebody hide the bayonet.

The neighbors assault the night air with an acoustic sing-along to "My Girl." Jack retaliates with a blast of Norwegian death metal, but there are friendly fire casualties: Kelly wakes up and screams, "I'm sleeping!" Master of the obvious, Jack retorts, "No, you're not!" With the Osbournes torn by internal dissent, the neighbors press their advantage with "He's Got the Whole World in His Hands." Jack answers back with his father's "War Pigs." Finally the Osbournes unleash their heavy artillery: Jack flings food from a balcony; Sharon shot-puts a rotting ham. Is this one of the War Pigs? The battlefield falls ominously quiet. "They said you were a crazy whore," whispers Kelly. "Well, they were right with that one," Sharon replies.

The two immaculately groomed, blonde Beverly Hills power walkers that turned up in the Osbournes' driveway one day made a mixed impression. Although they looked like two kids who had dared one another to ring the bell on the haunted house, they did invite Sharon to join them on their morning walks. Even though Sharon accepted the invitation in a tone of voice that suggested she'd rather drink a bottle of tacks, the power-walkers left on good terms. It wasn't until they reached the street and searched their memories that their faces fell. Ozzy Osbourne . . . wasn't he known for throwing raw meat? Killing animals? When last seen, they looked as though they'd had second thoughts about playing welcome wagon.

MOM WEARS
THE PANTS

Whether it's *All in the Family, Everybody Loves Raymond,* or *The Simpsons,* the husband may be a blowhard, but we all know who holds things together at home. Things are no different at the Osbournes'.

We got the message that this was a different sort of television mom when we heard Sharon swearing off housework: "Martha Stewart can lick my scrotum." She considers, "Do I have a scrotum?" Of course she does, in a jar upstairs: Billy Corgan's.

Still, when Jack and Kelly's lifestyles seem to have gotten out of control, it's Sharon who convenes a family meeting. Sharon wants to instill discipline, but even Ozzy lacks it: He continually gets up to leave until Sharon makes him sit. Kelly pleads for understanding from her parents: "Me and Jack have been brought up differently from everyone else." Ozzy, perplexed by this statement, looks as though he's thinking, *Different how?* Jack adds that their situation differs even from that of other musicians' children because no one else takes their kids on the road. Sharon explains that she made this decision so that the Osbournes could be a family. Kelly softens and says, "I wouldn't have it any other way." She then admits to being "verbally abused" in school by students who "still can't get over the fact . . . that Dad bit the head off a bat." Ozzy asks if Kelly would like home schooling. His question is met with silence, a silence that spread across the country as viewers everywhere were paralyzed by the thought of Ozzy Osbourne teaching their kids.

Sharon's most aggressive act of parental discipline occurs when she finds a hidden bottle of Jack Daniel's in Jack's room. She goes into the bathroom to pee in the bottle to teach the owner a lesson. If anything could keep a person off of whiskey for life, it probably would be associating it with a mouthful of your mom's pee. All parents take note.

A truism from the school of effective parenting is "do not overreact to your children's behavior." Sharon may have missed that chapter. On one occasion Sharon, due to Kelly's incessant use of the word *vagina*, tells Kelly they should have named her *Vagina Osbourne*. Kelly, seeking revenge, licks her finger and then wipes it beneath Sharon's nose. Not to be outdone, Sharon reaches down the front of her pants, feels around a bit, then extends a finger and chases Kelly, who flees screaming. Viewers everywhere do likewise. Like children everywhere, Kelly naively resists parental discipline. "She stuck her finger in her vagina and she's trying to wipe it on me!" she shrieks. If they had named Kelly *Vagina*, that would have been a confusing sentence.

As the show's executive producer, Sharon has final say as to what does and does not make it onto the air. MTV has said that the Osbournes have the ultimate right to call "cut" if there is something they definitely do not want captured on video or if they're simply "not in the mood to be on display." If the "finger chase" made it in, can you imagine the stuff Sharon actually flagged?

To be fair, Ozzy has tried, however feebly, to do his part in keeping order. Even the onetime master of mayhem understands that chaos and platinum record sales are not the most important ingredients for good parenting. Despite his lack of a sterling parenting pedigree, Ozzy has not shied away from setting limits with his kids and giving them honest advice. Ozzy says that, as a parent, he has always tried to be "rigorously honest."

Some of the rules Ozzy has tried to enforce:

The kids have a 2:30 A.M. curfew. (Frequently disobeyed.)

He insists that the kids not get drunk or do drugs. (Constantly disobeyed.)

He warns them to use a condom if they have sex. (Hopefully not the same one.)

Though Ozzy didn't have any compunction about giving Jack a bayonet, his cautious parenting gene kicks in when Jack shows him a small knife someone gave him. Ozzy takes the knife from Jack and hides it in their pantry closet. Jack has a tantrum. Ozzy explains that he is worried that one of his children's antics will get them all deported. Furious, Jack finally relents and gives Ozzy the knife. Ozzy hides it in a fruit bowl, perhaps assuming that it's the one place the pizza-loving Jack will never look.

UPSTAGED BY PETS

Who'd ever have thought there'd come a day when the animals in Ozzy's household would be more destructive than their owner? The role usually played by a lovable sitcom pooch like *Frasier*'s Eddie is shared by seven in the Osbourne pack: Minnie, the "top diva," is a four-year-old Pomeranian; Maggie, "heroin chic," is a Japanese Chin, as is the "neurotic" Crazy Baby; Pipi is a black Pomeranian owned by Aimee (wouldn't it make a great episode to hold Pipi hostage without food or water until Aimee came out?) Then there are the Chihuahuas: "Gay" Martini is a year old; Lulu, the grunting "seal," is three. Finally, there's Lola, Jack's "big, boisterous, adorable," scene-stealing bulldog.

With seven nonhousebroken dogs taking care of business, the Osbourne mansion has become, in Ozzy's words, "like bleeping Dr. Dolittle's bleeping house." No wonder when Kelly called from a pet shop, Ozzy broke down and begged Sharon not to allow another animal in the house. Although Sharon promised with all her heart, something in her voice told us Ozzy'd better get ready to share the litter box.

Lola's destruction of a chair cushion inspired one of Sharon's better lines. When Jack called the dog situation "dysfunctional," Sharon snapped, "Excuse me, that bleeping chair is dysfunctional." When Sharon recommended sending Lola to boot camp, Jack looked concerned. We can guess what he was thinking: *First the dogs, then me.*

"I'm not picking up another turd," Ozzy proclaimed. "I'm a rock star." Nevertheless, he seemed outraged when Sharon hired the dog therapist, Tamara. "You don't need a therapist," he declared. "You need to get up at seven and open the bleeping door."

Tamara endured Ozzy's complaints and was inches from a dignified exit when suddenly Lola peed on the carpet right in front of her. Well, at least she helped Lola get over her penis envy.

On most sitcoms, a reliance on cute pets is usually a sign of a creative drought. But clearly that's only the case if dog poop is an off-camera presence rather than

a featured player. Despite constantly screaming about having to clean up poop, Ozzy obviously loves the dogs, as evidenced by frequent shots of him and the dogs tongue kissing. If the ASPCA picketed him for the bat episode, surely they can do something about this?

When Jack's dog Lola triumphantly returns home after having been given away, the former pinnacle of the genre, Ross's reunion with his monkey, seems suddenly quaint in comparison. We're treated to a heartwarming love montage of Jack and Lola, the two of them kissing, swimming, cuddling, hugging. It's the most romantic cinematic experience since *Love Story* or *Ryan's Song*. Then Lola gets out of the pool, coughs a few times, and vomits white puke all over the deck. Sorry, Jack; maybe Lola wasn't quite ready for the commitment.

The dogs weren't the only fourfooted family members to cause trouble; the cats did their share, too. The news that Puss, the cat, had contracted herpes brought a look of terror to Ozzy's face and probably had the same effect on every dog he'd ever kissed. FYI: Feline herpesvirus 1

(FHV-1) is a very common disease in cats. Approximately 50 to 70 percent of adult cats have antibodies to the virus and the infection rate can be up to 100 percent in susceptible unvaccinated cats. While any cat can be infected, the incidence is higher in situations where large numbers of cats are housed together, such as in catteries, shelters, and boarding facilities. It's not clear which description best suits the Osbournes'.

Puss was almost single-handedly responsible for the long-term incapacitation of one of rock's biggest acts. When Puss escaped into the backyard, *Osbournes* fans were treated to what may well be the oddest chase scene ever filmed. Ozzy, putting his fractured leg at great risk, crept after Puss, calling her a "dumb shit mother-bleeper" and threatening to hit her with his walking stick. Ozzy later explained that he worried that coyotes would get Puss. This is not just Ozzy being weird: For you non–Los Angelenos, cats get carried off by coyotes all the time. Anyone familiar with Ozzy's track record might suggest that Puss would be better off taking her chances with the coyotes.

Another nail-biting moment came when a panicked cat, perhaps responding to some deep biological memory, climbed atop an antique mirror and refused to come down. The Osbourne women, Aimee and Melinda included, laughed and screamed while the accident-prone Ozzy teetered precariously on the edge of a bureau. From all the fuss, you'd think Ozzy was hunting the creature in *Alien.* An eager Jack, who unlike his father has never killed a cat, eagerly handed Ozzy bludgeoning instruments along with the helpful advice, "Hit it with this." Ozzy finally shook the mirror hard enough to bring the cat down. The clan scattered, screaming, as the cat scrambled to safety, no doubt worried that all the stress would bring on another herpes outbreak.

"For every Ozzy Osbourne, there's a million more that don't get that break."

SPECIAL GUEST STAR...

A variety of acquaintances, both casual and intimate, have contributed memorable moments to *The Osbournes*. Although the biggest fuss over *Lord of the Rings* star Elijah Wood and his sister, Hannah, was made by Lola, the bulldog, who greeted their arrival with a big steaming soft-serve on the floor, the Osbournes and the Woods are actually very close. Kelly and Hannah are good friends, and Elijah, too, is a frequent visitor to the mansion. By now, they have undoubtedly had many opportunities to clean up after the Osbourne pack. Wonder if they still cheerily whistle while they work? Cleaning up Lola's "aliens" looks like a chore that gets old fast. Jack's one on-screen attempt to do so resulted in a quick retreat, accompanied by the almost admiring groan, "That's tough!" Elijah was the one to ask the obvious question: How did such a brute wind up with a name like Lola? Maybe Ozzy once tried to eat Ray Davies?

Hopefully Elijah didn't take it personally when Ozzy responded to their introduction with a no-look handshake and walked away while Elijah was in midsentence. It's not just that Ozzy's hard to impress: Careful viewing of *The Osbournes* reveals that Ozzy greets almost everyone this way—everyone, that is, except for his fans.

No houseguest since Kato Kaelin stirred more trouble than Jason Dill. A friend whom Jack described as a professional skater, T-shirt maker, and "golden god in Japan" was clearly meant to be *The Osbournes'* version of *Real World's* Puck meets *Seinfeld's* Kramer.

Much was made of Ozzy's bewilderment over Jason's presence at the mansion. Ozzy had no idea who Jason was or what he was doing there. Ozzy's best guess was that Jason worked for him. When Ozzy, seated at his usual kitchen perch, sarcastically asked Jason if he was in Jason's seat, Jason took him seriously and generously permitted Ozzy to stay. An aggravated Ozzy eventually declared that if Jason was to be a long-term tenant, "I want bleeping rent."

Jason appeared to cause almost as much property damage as the dogs. He melted a timer on the griddle, creating a mess that resisted every effort to clean it. His late-night parties with the Osbourne kids resulted in, among other calamities, the unveiling of a naked fat man on a family program. Worse, when Sharon discovered Jason's whiskey bottle, Kelly had to wrestle it out of her mother's hand before before she could pee in it.

Behind the scenes, it was another story. Kelly was dismayed that Jason, whom she describes as "one of the nicest people I know," was depicted as a freeloading slob. Jason himself denies responsibility for Ozzy's failure to recognize him. He claims that he's been introduced to Ozzy on a number of occasions, but Ozzy always forgets. Exhibit A in Jason's defense: Ozzy has been known to forget his own age.

Elijah Wood

THE HOLIDAY SPECIAL

The holiday episode is one of the most cherished staples of any television show. It's Thanksgiving and the Osbournes have invited the entire viewing audience to their table. A classic American scene—until Ozzy bellows "Thanksgiving means bleep-all to me!" thereby destroying the holiday mood but winning over Native Americans everywhere. The next time Jack begs America to, as he puts it, "sling us a green card," he'd better hope this little scene has faded from memory.

Nowhere is the distinctive Osbourne blend of the familiar and the bizarre more apparent than during holiday observances. One moment Sharon tells Ozzy that she loves Christmas because the family can eat together and she and Ozzy can have a nice quiet evening at home. The next moment she agrees with Ozzy that that will never happen and they'll probably just call each other bastards and call it a night.

Even Ozzy seems amazed by the state of affairs in his household. Worrying over Sharon's latest Gucci shopping spree, Ozzy remembers how different Christmas was when he was a kid. All he would ever get was an old sock, some pennies, and maybe an apple or orange. It's amazing how $70 million changes everything.

At one point, Kelly confesses to the camera that she hates Christmas. She complains that it always ends sitting at a table with your family arguing about stupid bleep.

At Christmas dinner, after Jack gives Kelly the finger, she tells him to get the stick out of his ass. An argument follows over whether she said "stick" or "dick." If this isn't arguing over "stupid bleep," nothing is. Christmas dinner culminates with Sharon applauding her daughter's dramatic exit from the table. Kelly says she's going to go to a movie, but Sharon forbids it. Kelly's staying in because it's "bleeping Christmas!"

The moment that best illustrates what makes an Osbourne Christmas comes when Ozzy wishes Sharon a merry Christmas, warmly embraces her, and tells her that he loves her. Then he adds, "Now bleep off." Okay, it may not be as touching as everyone singing "Silent Night" by candlelight, but it's good television.

THE THIRD ACT✝

"Okay, there are definitely, definitely no third acts in American lives."

The Osbourne clan knocked the Enron scandal off of the front page of the *New York Times* business section with the announcement of their agreement with MTV for a second season. The article made it clear that the negotiations were some of the most difficult that MTV had ever been engaged in, and, unlike other networks, MTV is used to dealing with crazy rock stars! Highlights of the negotiations included the Osbournes' requesting a new house (perhaps all the dog-poop and Jason Dill stains didn't come out), lifetime psychotherapy for all their cats and dogs (God forbid they should send Jack), the Osbournes' saying they would sign their contracts in blood, and the threat of other networks looking to poach the show away from MTV. MTV also affirmed that the Osbournes had the most powerful tool at their disposal: They could shut down production if they thought the children were being upset in any way. After Kelly wrenched a bottle of Jack Daniel's away from her mother as she tried to fill it with pee, a guy with a camera is going to be upsetting?

For fans, the best part of the deal, other than twenty new episodes, is that the Osbournes retained the right to create new shows from outtakes! We may finally see some of the stuff that couldn't be shown on MTV (or in a God-fearing country).

THE 2,195TH STAR ON THE HOLLYWOOD WALK OF FAME BELONGS TO OZZY, APRIL 2002

Ozzy, the working-class outcast from Birmingham, has reached the pinnacle of acceptance in his native England. He sang for Queen Elizabeth and other members of Britain's royal household at the celebration of the Queen's Golden Jubilee. It should be no surprise to anyone who's followed Queen Elizabeth's reign that she's a huge Sabbath fan.

An ecstatic crowd cheered the Osbourne clan as they gathered for the unveiling of Ozzy's star on Hollywood's Walk of Fame. Ozzy was introduced as a man "who almost single-handedly revolutionized the world of rock music . . . the prince of bleeping darkness." Marilyn Manson, an obvious descendant of Ozzy's shock-rock persona, said at the ceremony, "This star right here proves that it's

quite obvious that Ozzy has managed to succeed while remaining insane and strangely happy despite his various crimes against God and nature."

When it came Ozzy's turn to address the crowd he said, "To say that this is an honor is not enough. This is just so overwhelming, with all of you turning out so early in the morning to see my old butt." Unfortunately for those who had actually shown up to see his butt, Ozzy restrained himself and kept it hidden in his pants. Never fear, the butt still appears regularly at his concerts. Ozzy's star is located directly in front of the Ripley's Believe It or Not museum of oddities, a place where it should feel right at home.

Wrapping up *The Osbournes'* first season, Ozzy lists things he's not proud of: a poor education, dyslexia, attention deficit disorder, drug and alcohol addiction, biting the head off a bat. He looks back over his life and finally concludes: "It could be worse . . . I could be Sting." (Maybe Nickelodeon will give *him* a reality show?)

But Ozzy summed it all up best when he said, "We're the Osbournes and I love it."

So do we.